WRITTEN BY HELEN BROWN

EDITED BY FRANCES EVANS

DESIGNED BY DERRIAN BRADDER

COVER DESIGN BY ANGIE ALLISON

STERLING CHILDREN'S BOOKS
New York

An Imprint of Sterling Publishing Co., Inc.
1166 Avenue of the Americas
New York, NY 10036

ISBN 978-1-4549-3952-8

For information about custom editions, special sales, and premium
and corporate purchases, please contact Sterling Special Sales
at 800-805-5489 or specialsales@sterlingpublishing.com.

Manufactured in China
Lot #:
2 4 6 8 10 9 7 5 3 1
01/20

sterlingpublishing.com

Cover artwork from www.shutterstock.com

With special thanks to Becca Wright

Picture credits
Front cover: Jordan Strauss/Invision/AP/Shutterstock
Back cover: Roger Kisby/Stringer/Getty Images for YouTube

Page 2–3, 34, 42, 43: Terence Patrick/CBS Photo Archive via Getty Images
Page 6, 11, 20–21, 56–57: Christopher Polk/REX/Shutterstock
Page 9: Kim Hee-Chul/EPA/REX/Shutterstock
Page 13, 23, 37: Han Myung-Gu/WireImage/Getty Images
Page 15, 25, 39, 47: Jordan Strauss/Invision/AP/Shutterstock
Page 33: Roger Kisby/Stringer/Getty Images for YouTube
Page 35: THE FACT/Imazins via Getty Images
Page 45: Dimitrios Kambouris/Getty Images for Michael Kors
Page 61: Scott Kowalchyk/CBS Photo Archive via Getty Images
Page 62–63: Chung Sung-Jun/Getty Images

QUEENS Of K-POP

BLACKPINK

STERLING CHILDREN'S BOOKS
New York

CONTENTS

COMING TOGETHER

When Jisoo, Jennie, Rosé, and Lisa debuted as a group in 2016, they captured the attention of people all around the world. Since then, they have gone from strength to strength, breaking world records and making history. Before they met, the girls had their own individual successes, but when they came together they created such powerful, inspirational music that they never looked back.

The group's first job was to decide on a band name, one that sent out a powerful message to the world. Fans felt that the girls' unique choice – BLACKPINK – made a statement on feminism today. The color pink is commonly associated with femininity so, by combining pink with the darkest color there is, black, the band was subtly undermining this stereotype.

The group's label, YG Entertainment, believed that the name conveyed how these four strong and intelligent women embodied not only beauty but also great talent. As Jennie sings in the opening lines of "Ddu-Du Ddu-Du," "I may look sweet, but I don't act like it".

BLACKPINK was the first girl group in six years to debut under YG Entertainment. Before them, 2NE1 had sold 66.5 million records and was one of the most successful and popular girl groups in South Korea. To this day, BLACKPINK remain the agency's only girl group and is currently managed by Jung Bo-kyung.

BLACKPINK IN YOUR AREA
BLACKPINK IN YOUR AREA
BLACKPINK IN YOUR AREA
BLACKPINK IN YOUR AREA
BLACKPINK IN YOUR AREA
BLACKPINK IN YOUR AREA
BLACKPINK IN YOUR AREA
BLACKPINK IN YOUR AREA

QUICK QUESTION
What are the big three K-pop agencies in South Korea?

Answer: SM Entertainment, JYP Entertainment and YG Entertainment

BLACKPINK's debut single album, *Square One*, was released on August 8th, 2016. The two singles from the album, "Whistle" and "Boombayah," charted immediately at numbers one and two on *Billboard*'s World Digital Songs Chart. The girls became the fastest music act to achieve this, which was an incredible accomplishment. "Whistle" also topped the digital, download, streaming, and mobile categories of the Gaon Chart in August 2016. To top it all, the band reached number one on the K-pop music video chart of China's biggest music-streaming website, QQ Music.

BLACKPINK's debut TV performance was aired on SBS's music show *Inkigayo* six days later. The girls performed both of the songs from their album and won first place. This win came only 13 days after their debut, which made BLACKPINK record holders again! They held the record for the quickest time in which a girl group had won on a music programme after their debut.

The potential for BLACKPINK to hit the global market was clear. In October 2018, YG Entertainment teamed up with Interscope Records and Universal Music Group to represent the band outside of Asia. This partnership helped to promote the band internationally. A few months later, BLACKPINK made their debut on US television with performances on *The Late Show with Stephen Colbert* and *Good Morning America*.

DID YOU KNOW?

In 2019, BLACKPINK performed on James Corden's *The Late Late Show*. The talk-show host thought they were brilliant and turned his Twitter into a fan account for the day.

Along with their epic dance moves and beautiful voices, every member of the band plays an instrument – and in some cases two! Jisoo plays the drums and guitar, Jennie plays the piano and flute, Rosé plays the piano and guitar, and Lisa plays the ukulele. This talent sets them apart from other K-pop groups and makes them even more accessible to their fans (known as Blinks) as they showcase their skills on YouTube.

Between them, the girls speak five languages fluently: Chinese, English, Japanese, Korean, and Thai. This ability to communicate internationally is another strength that ties them together.

> "As a group with a multicultural background, we have the advantage of being able to speak language freely ... Our music seems to be enjoyed by everyone regardless of race, age and gender."
> – Lisa, 2019

JISOO
lead vocalist, visual

JENNIE
main rapper, vocalist

ROSÉ
main vocalist, lead dancer

LISA
main dancer, lead rapper, sub-vocalist, maknae

♥ ♥ ♥ ♥ ♥ ♥ ♥

"Maknae" is the term given to the youngest member of a K-pop group.

♥ ♥ ♥ ♥ ♥ ♥ ♥

♥ ♥ ♥ ♥ ♥ ♥ ♥

"Visual" is the term given to the best-looking member of a K-pop group.

♥ ♥ ♥ ♥ ♥ ♥ ♥

JISOO

" **I never dream to be anything not possible.** "

Name:
Kim Ji-soo

Also known as:
Jisoo, Chi Choo, Jichu

Date of birth:
January 3rd, 1995

Star sign:
Capricorn

Birthplace:
Seoul, South Korea

Height:
5 feet, 3 inches

Education:
School of Performing
Arts High School, Seoul

Languages:
Korean, Japanese,
basic Chinese

Early career:
Became a YG Entertainment
trainee in 2011

Joined BLACKPINK:
Third member to be revealed
on June 15th, 2016

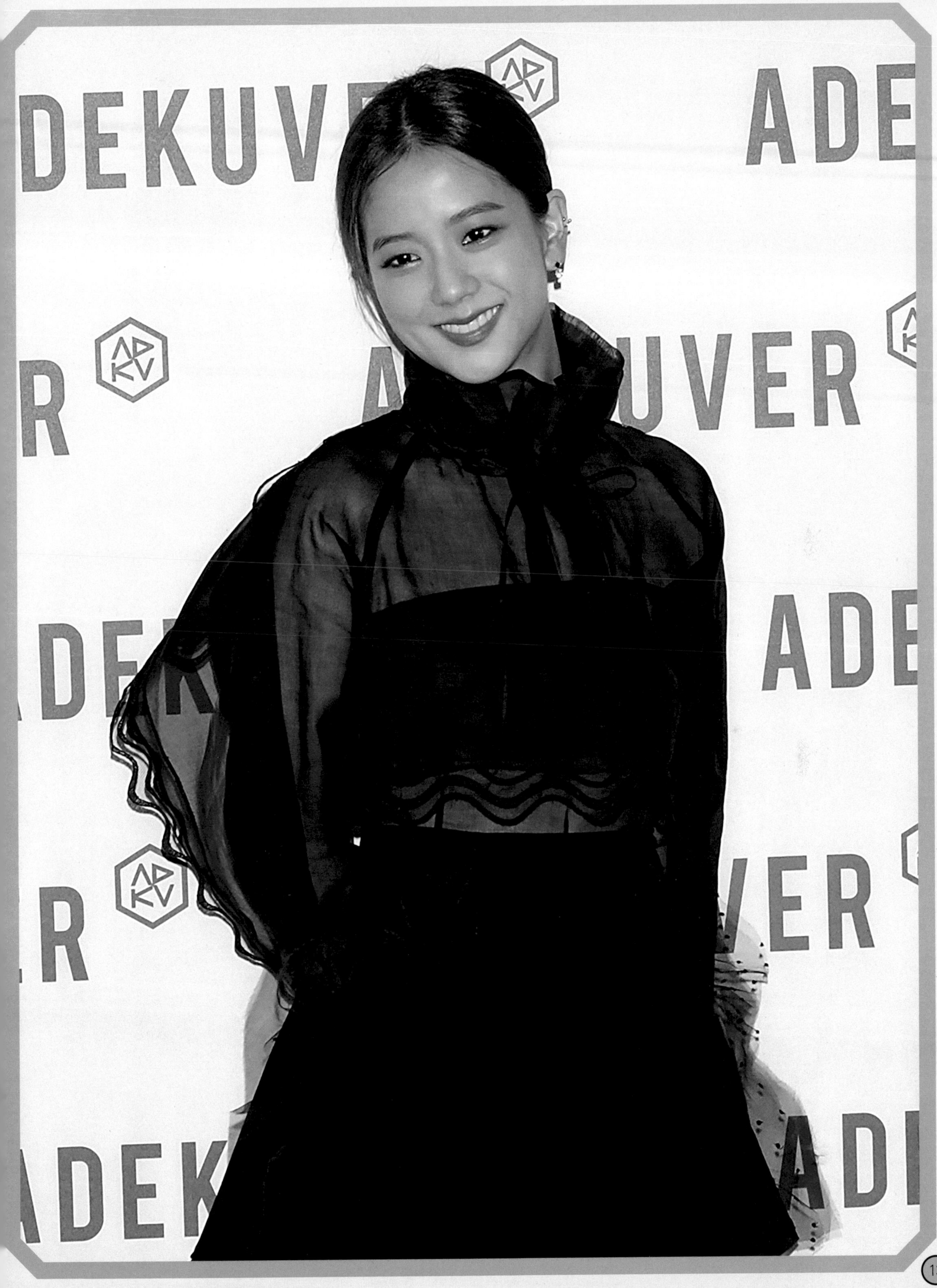
DEKUVER
UVER
VER

> "Don't rely on what others tell you to do, have a firm grasp and do something you like according to your own initiative."

JISOO
JISOO
JISOO
JISOO
JISOO
JISOO
JISOO
JISOO

> "All of us at the company went to go see a concert together, and [someone asked me] 'Have you ever thought about trying to be a celebrity?' But the fact that I was a trainee had not been officially announced yet, so I had to just say I wasn't interested."

EARLY DAYS

Kim Ji-soo, better known as Jisoo, was born in the small city of Gunpo, Gyeonggi Province, South Korea. Jisoo studied at the School of Performing Arts High School and is trilingual. She speaks Korean, Japanese, and basic Chinese, but is the only member of the group who does not speak fluent English.

Not a lot is known about Jisoo's parents, but rumor has it that her father is the CEO of Rainbow Bridge World, the South Korean entertainment company that manages girl group Mamamoo. Jisoo is the youngest of three siblings and has an older brother and sister. They are a close family — Jisoo has spoken about her childhood and playing with her siblings. She especially loved to play Beyblades (spinning top toys) with her older brother.

THE BEGINNINGS

Jisoo has loved to sing ever since she was a young child. She would often sing and dance in front of her family at gatherings, and they would shower her with praise. This gave Jisoo the confidence to pursue a career in singing, so she began auditioning.

She joined YG Entertainment as a trainee in August 2011, at the age of 16. On an episode of the South Korean talk show *Radio Star* in 2017, Jisoo claimed that she was scouted by SM Entertainment when she was at a YG Entertainment Concert. However, as she had already signed a contract with YG Entertainment, she could not accept the offer of training with SM Entertainment.

It was clear that Jisoo had the looks and talent of a potential star. She put in a lot of hours to make it to the top and trained with YG Entertainment for five years before being revealed as the third member of BLACKPINK in 2016.

"Before we debuted, we only wanted to stand on stage and have fans. We often thought, 'Would people like us?'"

Jisoo now feels a sense of responsibility to ensure that the band meets the expectations of Blinks, who continuously love and support them. She focuses on different parts of their performances to make sure they satisfy their fans. She is aware that, even if the girls prepare everything perfectly, it's never certain that a performance will run smoothly.

CONFIDENCE, CHARISMA, CHARM

Jisoo has grown in confidence and, as the oldest member of the group, she often takes the lead in interviews as well as on stage.

Despite being the eldest in years, Jisoo has all the traits of the youngest member – she's very silly and loves to make fun of herself. Blinks go wild when they see her on TV entertainment shows because her bright and fun personality shines through on screen.

JISOO
JISOO
JISOO
JISOO
JISOO
JISOO
JISOO
JISOO

DID YOU KNOW?

Jisoo is the only member who hasn't shed "happy tears" at an awards show. That isn't to say that she doesn't care; as the girls have revealed, she has a soft, emotional side.

JISOO'S ADVICE FOR LIFE

"You cannot disobey the truth of life."

"Life is all about timing."

"Life is not easy, there are so many crossroads ... that's our life."

WHAT DO THE GIRLS SAY ABOUT JISOO?

Jisoo is a confident member of the band. She is always making the girls laugh and is known as the "mood maker" of the group.

JENNIE

Jennie says that if she was a guy she would date Jisoo because she makes her laugh.

LISA

"Jisoo is so funny. When I'm with her I can always be happy and just keep laughing."

Jisoo loves dogs and owns a cute, white Maltese dog called Dalgom, also known as Dalgomie.

Jisoo cuddles Dalgom at night to help with her sleep paralysis and nightmares.

At the last count, Jisoo has a total of nine piercings – four on her left ear and five on her right ear.

Jisoo has admitted that she is the worst dancer of the group. She says that her "dancing skill is still lacking – I can dance better when we practice."

Jisoo spends her free time playing games and loves to play with Jennie.

TEN FACTS ABOUT JISOO

Jisoo has a variety of special talents. She can play the drums and piano, and has taken up tae kwon do.

Jisoo says she can balance anything on her head (except her dog, Dalgom!).

Jisoo is obsessed with Pikachu (the fictional character from Pokémon). She owns a lot of Pikachu merchandise, including a hat, a onesie, and plenty of cuddly toys.

Jisoo loves to read and is known as the band's bookworm. She once said that she feels "a small joy" when she reads a book.

Jisoo does not love all animals and is afraid of rodents. She is most scared of rabbits and hamsters and was actually bitten by a hamster as a child.

BLINKS

BLACKPINK has hundreds of thousands of supporters who are some of the most dedicated fans in the world.

"The meaning of Blink comes from the beginning and ending letters of BL-ACKP-INK, meaning we're together from start to end."
– BLACKPINK, 2016

The signature phrase from the group's debut song, "Boombayah," is "BLACKPINK in your area." The girls often use it on Twitter to announce plans for new shows to their fans. Jennie says that the band are "blessed" to be leading the K-pop movement.

"It's such an honor to be receiving so much love, and we never want to take this moment for granted."
– Jennie, 2018

The girls say that setting up their fan club has been one of the highlights of their careers; they never imagined in their wildest dreams that their music would reach out to so many people around the world. The girls themselves have a multicultural background, coming from New Zealand, Australia, Thailand, and South Korea. Jennie, Lisa, and Rosé also speak English fluently, which has helped fans outside Asia connect with, and feel closer to, the band.

Being able to understand and communicate properly with Blinks is vital to BLACKPINK's success. BLACKPINK use English not only to chat with their foreign fans but also to introduce them to Korean culture. The girls are aware and respectful of all the different cultures they connect with, and they encourage fans to recognize and be considerate of these differences, too.

This inclusivity is reflected in the band's concerts as well. BLACKPINK have shown support for their LGBTQ+ fanbase by holding rainbow flags while on tour in the Philippines. At the moment, same-sex marriage is not legally recognized in South Korea, so these small acts make every fan feel accepted, proud, and loved by the band.

QUICK QUESTION
BLACKPINK take Blinks behind the scenes in a reality TV series. What is the series called?

HOW TO GET CLOSE TO THE GIRLS

Be prepared at all times
Arrive early to a show or hang around afterward to increase your chances of meeting the girls. Don't forget to bring your phone for an impromptu selfie.

Go to a fansign
Fansigns are the perfect place to meet the girls and also have your albums signed. Generally, there are two types of fansigns – first-come-first-served and lottery events. Check the rules as sometimes it's the first 100 people to buy the new album who get tickets, and other times it's down to luck.

Write letters
At fansign events you have the opportunity to give the girls handwritten letters. Some Blinks attempt to give gifts, but the girls aren't allowed to accept them as they can be seen as bribes. However, in early 2019, a Blink offered Jennie a small toy pig that she accepted while making a *ssh* gesture – as if to say it was their little secret!

Go big or go home
Get noticed at a concert by shouting the loudest. In March 2019, a fan shouted a marriage proposal to Jennie when the band was on stage in Manila, Philippines. In response, Jennie pointed to her fourth finger and put out her hands, suggesting they should give her a ring!

Know when it's time to go
Selfie? Check. Declaration that you're a dedicated Blink? Check. Now leave the girls to get to their next show. Some Blinks can cause huge commotion at events – such as invading personal space and privacy. It's much nicer to meet the girls on their own terms.

♥ ♥ ♥ ♥ ♥ ♥ ♥

"Our fans from around the world, we are so grateful for their love and support."
– Jisoo, 2018

♥ ♥ ♥ ♥ ♥ ♥ ♥

"It made us happy to think that a connection had been forged between us and our fans."
– Jennie, 2018

♥ ♥ ♥ ♥ ♥ ♥ ♥

"We definitely appreciate the fact that many people look forward to our music and stage performances."
– Rosé, 2018

♥ ♥ ♥ ♥ ♥ ♥ ♥

"Thank you Blinks around the world that keep cheering for us for the whole time."
– Lisa, 2018

♥ ♥ ♥ ♥ ♥ ♥ ♥

ACCOUNTS TO FOLLOW

WEBSITE
♥ blackpinkofficial.com ♥
The official website featuring all the music videos, tour information, concept photos and much more.

YOUTUBE
♥ BLACKPINK ♥
Short videos of behind-the-scenes footage.

VLIVE
♥ BLACKPINK ♥
A video streaming service that the girls use to broadcast live videos and chat with fans.

INSTAGRAM
♥ @blackpinkofficial ♥
The official account for sharing concept photos, teaser videos, and messages from the group.

♥ @sooyaa__ ♥
The official account for Jisoo

♥ @jennierubyjane ♥
The official account for Jennie

♥ @lesyeuxdenini ♥
Jennie's second account for personal photography.

♥ @roses_are_rosie ♥
The official account for Rosé

♥ @lalalalisa_m ♥
The official account for Lisa

FACEBOOK
♥ @BLACKPINKOFFICIAL ♥
The official account for sharing posts and connecting with the group and the fans.

JENNIE

"BLACKPINK is number one."

Name:
Kim Jennie

Also known as:
Jennie, Jendeukie,
Human Chanel, Nini

Date of birth:
January 16th, 1996

Star sign:
Capricorn

Birthplace:
Gyeonggi, South Korea

Height:
5 feet, 4 inches

Education:
ACG Parnell College,
New Zealand

Languages:
Korean, Japanese, English

Early career:
Became a YG Entertainment
trainee in 2010

Joined BLACKPINK:
First member to be revealed
on June 1st, 2016

> **"At first my friends helped me and shared their notes with me. Now, I'm more comfortable with English than I used to be."**

JENNIE
JENNIE
JENNIE
JENNIE
JENNIE
JENNIE
JENNIE
JENNIE

> **"After receiving great support from my mom, I came back to Korea, ready to make my future through my favorite music."**

EARLY DAYS

Kim Jennie, known as Jennie, was born in Gyeonggi, a small town in Seoul, South Korea. Jennie comes from a hardworking family — her mother is a director of a media company and her father is the owner of a hospital. She is an only child, so thinks of the BLACKPINK girls as her sisters, especially Jisoo, to whom she is very close. Jennie is trilingual and can speak Japanese, Korean, and English fluently.

When Jennie was nine years old, she was sent to live in Auckland, New Zealand for five years as a study-abroad student. Jennie first appeared on screen in a 2006 documentary, *English, Must Change To Survive*, and spoke about her experiences of learning English and her life in New Zealand.

THE BEGINNINGS

Jennie listened to a lot of K-pop while she was in New Zealand and started to dream of becoming an entertainer. She told her mom that she wanted to pursue a career in music and moved back to Seoul in 2010. She had a successful audition with YG Entertainment the same year and was signed up as a trainee for the next six years.

During this time, Jennie became one of YG Entertainment's best-known trainees and was featured in songs by several other bands. She first gained the attention of fans after her 2012 appearance in G-Dragon's music video for "That XX." She also performed on several songs by other YG Entertainment artists, such as Lee Hi's "Special."

In 2016, she became the main rapper and vocalist of BLACKPINK. When Jennie was confirmed as an official member, fans were thrilled to hear that she was finally making her debut.

FASHION FORWARD

Jennie is the most fashion-conscious member of the group and is often seen at catwalks dressed in brands such as Gucci, Lanvin, Chanel, and Givenchy. In October 2018, she attended her first Chanel show at Paris Fashion Week, sitting on the front row next to Pharrell Williams and Pamela Anderson.

GOING SOLO

In October 2018, Jennie's official solo debut was announced. The track "Solo" was revealed during BLACKPINK's World Tour "In Your Area" in Seoul ahead of its release on November 12th.

"Solo" showcased Jennie's adaptability as both a rapper and a singer. It also established her as a fashion icon – she wore more than 20 outfits in the three-minute clip! Jennie was the first member to release a solo record and was amazed when it hit number one on *Billboard*'s World Digital Song Sales Chart.

"As all of our members have their own personality, taste in music, and style, it'll be great if we can showcase all of our individual strengths through these solo projects."

JENNIE
JENNIE
JENNIE
JENNIE
JENNIE
JENNIE
JENNIE
JENNIE

DID YOU KNOW?

In June 2018, Jennie was announced as Chanel Korea's brand ambassador.

JENNIE'S WORDS OF APPRECIATION

"I am so grateful."

"BLACKPINK is the best with four members."

"We will continue to work hard to [receive] much love and support from fans."

WHAT DO THE GIRLS SAY ABOUT JENNIE?

Jennie is the glue that holds BLACKPINK together. The "black" in BLACKPINK is said to represent her. She loves to wear black clothes, which reflects her edgy stage personality.

LISA

"Jennie is so cool! Even though she's cool, whenever I sometimes get to see her sweet side, she's so cute."

JISOO

"Jennie is the one I leaned toward when I first joined here. Her dance, rap, and singing skills are beyond good. She's so multitalented. More than that, she is the decision maker in our team."

Jennie made history as the first solo female K-pop act to top the World Digital Song Sales Chart as a lead artist with her track "Solo." "Solo" also became the most-viewed music video by a female K-pop solo artist in the first 24 hours of its release.

Jennie was voted one of the most beautiful faces of 2017.

Jennie likes taking photos with retro cameras.

Jennie hates traveling and suffers from motion sickness.

Jennie has two dogs, Kai and Kuma. Kai, a white Cocker Spaniel, is shy and doesn't like to play much, whereas Pomeranian Kuma is more outgoing.

TEN FACTS ABOUT JENNIE

Jennie's hero is Rihanna. She once said, "My number one idol will always be Rihanna. She has everything I want to have."

After claiming that one of her talents was eating potato chips without making a sound, Jennie was caught out when she appeared on the variety show *Knowing Brothers*. They offered her a potato chip, but she made a crunching noise while eating it!

Jennie loves milk-flavored ice cream.

One of Jennie's favorite things to do is to stay at home with her family and eat strawberries.

Jennie's favorite colors are ... black and pink!

JOURNEY THROUGH MUSIC

BLACKPINK has released many albums since their debut in 2016 and showcased how versatile and talented they are.

Korean single albums

SQUARE ONE (2016)

Square One was the band's first single album, released when they debuted in 2016. Its two tracks, "Whistle" and "Boombayah," were huge commercial successes and introduced a new generation of K-pop stars to the world.

In South Korea, "Whistle" topped the Gaon Digital Chart. It entered at number two on *Billboard*'s World Digital Songs Chart in the US, with "Boombayah" entering at number one. BLACKPINK became the fastest act to hit number one on the chart, and only the third to hold the top two positions after Psy and Big Bang.

SQUARE TWO (2016)

Square Two was released later in 2016. The album had three tracks: "Playing With Fire," "Stay," and the acoustic version of "Whistle." "Playing With Fire" became their second single to hit number one on *Billboard*'s World Digital Songs Chart. The album ranked number 13 on *Billboard*'s Top Heatseekers Chart and number two on the US World Albums Chart.

Korean mini-albums

SQUARE UP (2018)

Square Up was BLACKPINK's first Korean mini-album and contained four tracks: "Ddu-Du Ddu-Du," "Forever Young," "Really," and "See U Later." "Ddu-Du Ddu-Du" spent three weeks at the top of the Gaon Chart and also became the group's first single to enter *Billboard*'s Hot 100 Chart, debuting and peaking at number 55. As of April 2019, the single has achieved a platinum certification for both streaming and downloads within South Korea.

KILL THIS LOVE (2019)

Kill This Love was the band's second Korean mini-album and featured five songs: "Kill This Love," "Don't Know What To Do," "Kick It," "Hope Not," and the remixed version of "Ddu-Du Ddu-Du." The EP received positive reviews and peaked at number 24 on *Billboard*'s 200 Albums Chart. "Kill This Love" reached number 41 on *Billboard*'s Hot 100 Chart. It was the group's third single in the chart, and it also extended their record of the most entries on the chart and of the longest-charting single by a South Korean girl group.

Japanese studio albums

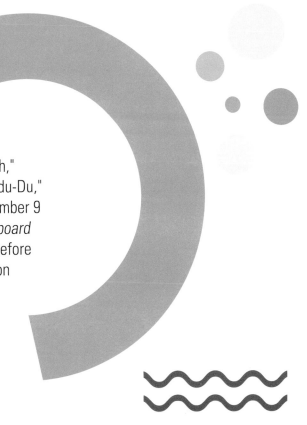

BLACKPINK IN YOUR AREA (2018)

This was the band's first Japanese studio album and was released digitially in November and physically in December 2018. The album included Japanese versions of nine of the group's singles: "Boombayah," "Whistle," "Playing With Fire," "Stay," "As If It's Your Last," "Ddu-Du Ddu-Du," "Forever Young," "Really," and "See U Later." The album debuted at number 9 on the Oricon Albums Chart in its first week, and at number 91 on *Billboard Japan*'s Top Download Albums. It stayed at the latter for two weeks before peaking at number 77 in its third week. It also debuted at number 12 on *Billboard Japan*'s Hot Albums and placed at number 9 on Top Albums Sales with 14,710 combined copies sold.

Japanese mini-albums

BLACKPINK (2017)

In May 2017, it was announced that BLACKPINK would debut in Japan that summer, holding a showcase in July at the Nippon Budokan arena in Tokyo and releasing a mini-album in August. This mini-album included Japanese versions of six of the group's singles: "Boombayah," "Whistle," "Playing With Fire," "Stay," "As If It's Your Last," and the acoustic version of "Whistle." It debuted at the top of the Oricon Daily Album Chart and BLACKPINK became only the third non-Japanese band with a debut release to record first place on the Oricon Weekly Chart since 2011.

RE: BLACKPINK (REPACKAGE) (2018)

In March 2018, the girls released a repackage of their debut Japanese mini-album, BLACKPINK. It came in three versions: a CD edition, a CD+DVD edition and a Playbutton version. The album featured the same contents as their Japanese mini-album plus performances from the "BLACKPINK PREMIUM DEBUT SHOWCASE". This included a special interview with the girls as well as a behind-the-scenes film of their photoshoot for the album's jacket.

Other releases

"SO HOT" (THEBLACKLABEL REMIX) (2017)

"So Hot" is a remix version of a song by the South Korean girl group Wonder Girls. BLACKPINK performed it during the 2017 *SBS Gayodaejun* before releasing it on SoundCloud and YouTube. It became the most-viewed live performance of the 2017 *SBS Gayodaejun* on YouTube with more than 20 million views, and it peaked at number three of the "Best Live Performances" at the event.

Singles

"WHISTLE" (2016)

This song is a combination of a minimalist hip-hop production and a pop composition. *Billboard*'s K-pop columnist Jeff Benjamin wrote that the song "brings together impassioned crooning and their youthful hip-hop delivery with minimal drum 'n' bass and an undeniable whistle hook." It has a laid-back, gimmicky tune, with the whistle motif being used to suggest both a love call and the rhythm of a beating heart. When the music video was released on YouTube, it gained nearly ten million views in just five days. The video established the group as strong performers; amid physically demanding choreography, Jennie and Lisa showcased their rapping skills, and Rosé and Jisoo delivered incredible vocals.

"BOOMBAYAH" (2016)

From the moment Jennie shouted "BLACKPINK in your area" it was clear that this tune was a classic. With booming bass lines and wailing sirens, the girls deliver a four-minute, fast-paced, electro-pop track with a powerful beat. The music video was directed by Seo Hyun-seung, whose credits include "I Am the Best" by 2NE1 and "Fantastic Baby" by Big Bang. The urban, street-style fashion in the video reflects the "good to be bad" concept of the song. As Lisa raps in the first verse, "I'm so hot I need a fan, I don't want a boy, I need a man."

"PLAYING WITH FIRE" (2016)

This tune puts a twist on a traditional love song with its funky dance beat. The lyrics are meaningful and raw, exploring feelings of love and heartbreak. Jennie admits that she had to draw on fiction to connect with the lyrics. She said that "the song portrays love as playing with fire, but I never had such an experience, so I turned to movies to understand the feelings of love." Jisoo added that, "All of us only had second-hand experiences."

"STAY" (2016)

"Stay" shows a different side of BLACKPINK. This song is a rare ballad, displaying Jennie and Lisa's softer rapping along with Jisoo and Rosé's acoustic melodies. The music video is serious and gloomy, as the girls express the pain of being in love and heartbreak of the person you love leaving. At the end of the video, they send off colored flares in the hope that their loved ones will see the lights.

"AS IF IT'S YOUR LAST" (2017)

This was the first and only original song to be released by the girls in 2017, and it did not disappoint. It was their most exciting and upbeat song to date. Jisoo commented that, until then, the group had only explored "BLACK" concepts whereas this single was a "PINK" concept. It had an energetic, Moombahton-inspired melody and passionate lyrics (a fusion of house music and reggae). The music video shows the girls dressed in bold outfits, dancing with delight against a yellow backdrop. The song was later featured in the DC Extended Universes film *Justice League*.

"DDU-DU DDU-DU" (2018)

This record-breaking anthem featured hard-hitting rap verses and dynamic trap beats. It brought a fresh sound to the genre, and the combination of rap, trap elements, and fierce dance moves sent a message to the world: BLACKPINK has arrived. The music video oozes confidence and girl-power from the moment Jennie appears sitting on a throne on a giant chessboard. She's followed by Lisa, who wields a pink hammer while money piles up behind her. Rosé is out of reach, as she swings in on a chandelier, and Jisoo stays true to her fashion-forward image by rocking a pink wig. The girls didn't have chart success in mind when they made "Ddu-Du Ddu-Du" – as Jennie says, "We were worried that fans might not like our new, stronger concept. But now we have the courage to try new things next time."

"KILL THIS LOVE" (2019)

This chart-topping single made waves for its inspiring content. Rosé said that "the title speaks for itself. It's a very empowering song." The song is about ending toxic love – love that hurts and makes you vulnerable and weak. As the girls sing, "while I force myself to cover my eyes, I need to bring an end to this love." They wanted to tell Blinks that love can be found within them. They encourage their fans to find love that makes them feel confident and comfortable. Upon release, the music video broke the YouTube record for the most views within 24 hours, reaching 56.7 million, and went on to gain hundreds of millions of views.

QUICK QUESTION

Which BLACKPINK music video gained more than 11 million views on YouTube, just 17 hours after its release, becoming the fastest music video to exceed 10 million views by a K-pop group?

Answer: 'As If It's Your Last'. They broke the record previously held by BTS's 'Not Today'.

CONQUERING THE WORLD

BLACKPINK has been pushing boundaries and making history ever since they dropped on to the music scene.

US DEBUT

In February 2019, BLACKPINK made their debut US performance during Grammy weekend at a private party for Universal Music Group — the biggest record label in the world. Celebrities and music industry executives attended the event, and watched the girls perform "Ddu-Du Ddu-Du" and their *Square Up* album track "Forever Young." The girls performed alongside 2019 Grammy nominees Post Malone, J Balvin and Ella Mai. It was a big moment for BLACKPINK.

Later that month, the girls performed on *The Late Show with Stephen Colbert*. The show featured a surprise appearance from Hollywood actor Bradley Cooper, and BLACKPINK closed it with a performance of "Ddu-Du Ddu-Du." Colbert even took a backstage selfie with the band afterward.

MAKING HISTORY

The girls made history when they became the first K-pop girl group to perform at Coachella, an annual music and arts festival held in California. Over 250,000 people attended, including A-list celebrities and world-famous musicians. Jisoo, Jennie, Rosé, and Lisa performed 13 songs, wearing sparkly dresses and two-piece sets that shimmered under the colorful lights as they showed off their signature moves. The production was impressive; the stage had multiple screens of varying sizes, and the girls made use of the unique setup by projecting out-of-this-world visuals and colorful lyrics to some of their songs, so the crowd could join in and sing along.

The girls were aware of how important their performance was, both for them and the K-pop industry. During the set, Rosé made a reference to the contrasts in culture between the USA and South Korea.

> **"Coming all the way from South Korea, we didn't know what to expect [...] you guys and us are totally from different worlds, but tonight, I think [that] music brings us [together] as one."**
> — Rosé, 2019

QUICK QUESTION

What was the opening song of BLACKPINK's Coachella set?

Answer: 'Ddu-Du Ddu-Du.'

Blinks loved every second of the girls' set, and the performance was live-streamed on a large screen in New York's Times Square. But it wasn't just fans who gave the show rave reviews. A writer for *NME* magazine wrote a glowing article, claiming that BLACKPINK's history-making Coachella debut was as impressive as they come.

"With Coachella well and truly conquered, in BLACKPINK's case, we're going to be seeing a lot more of them and, on this showing, it'd be no shock to see them topping the whole bill in a few years' time."

– *NME* magazine, 2019

It was a breath of fresh air to see these female idols making waves and getting the recognition they deserved internationally.

COLLABORATIONS

In 2019, BLACKPINK collaborated with English singer-songwriter Dua Lipa on "Kiss and Make Up." The song was meant to be on Dua's first album, and she wanted it to be a collaboration but struggled to find the right artist for it. When Dua met the girls at a concert, the idea of a collaboration between them was born.

"When I was last in Singapore, I also went to Seoul, and Jennie and Lisa from BLACKPINK came to the show and I met them, and we hung out and we got on really well. I thought I should send the song to BLACKPINK and see if they'd be into joining it."

– Dua Lipa, 2019

The song helped BLACKPINK to reach new audiences around the world and has over 230 million streams on Spotify. It debuted at number 36 on the UK Singles Chart, making BLACKPINK the first female K-pop group to reach the top 40 on the chart.

The girls expressed how grateful they were that Dua reached out to work together. They've said that their future dream collaborations would be the American singer-songwriter Billie Eilish and American rapper and singer Tyga.

ENDORSEMENTS

Only three weeks after their debut in 2016, BLACKPINK placed second behind EXO (another huge K-pop band) for brand reputation, based on a study by the Korea Institute of Corporate Reputation. The chief of the research lab described it as a "first."

Since then, the girls have cemented their status as one of K-pop's most in-demand groups when it comes to endorsements. BLACKPINK became ambassadors for Incheon Main Customs in May 2017, and over the last few years they have endorsed and collaborated with several high-end brands, including Puma, Reebok, Louis Vuitton, Dior Cosmetics, and Sprite Korea.

In November 2018, BLACKPINK became a regional brand ambassador for a Singaporean e-commerce platform, Shopee. This was part of their partnership with YG Entertainment in seven different countries: Indonesia, Singapore, Malaysia, Philippines, Thailand, Vietnam, and Taiwan.

ROSÉ

" Dream big when you can and enjoy it. "

Name:
Roseanne Park /
Park Chae-young

Also known as:
Rosé, Rosie, Pasta

Date of birth:
February 11th, 1997

Star sign:
Aquarius

Birthplace:
Auckland, New Zealand

Height:
5 feet, 6 inches

Education:
Canterbury Girls
Secondary College,
Australia

Languages:
Korean, Japanese, English

Early career:
Became a YG Entertainment
trainee in 2012

Joined BLACKPINK:
The last member to be revealed
on June 22nd, 2016

"In Australia, I didn't think that there was much of a chance for me to become a singer – especially to become a K-pop star … I was living so far from the country that it never really occurred to me as a possibility."

ROSÉ
ROSÉ
ROSÉ
ROSÉ
ROSÉ
ROSÉ
ROSÉ
ROSÉ

"My father is the one who realized my love for music, and he let me go to the audition. Before that, I enjoyed music as a hobby, but when I realized more about my talent, my passion got bigger."

EARLY DAYS

Roseanne Park, better known as Rosé, was born in Auckland, New Zealand. However, her family moved to Australia when Rosé was seven years old, so she was educated in Melbourne, including attending Canterbury Girls Secondary College.

Rosé has one sister, Alice, who is four years older than her and is the spitting image of fellow bandmate Jisoo! Alice, like their father, is a lawyer, while their mother is a businesswoman. Rosé is very close to her family, especially her mother. When Rosé was on *King of Masked Singer*, a South Korean singing competition, she dedicated her performance to her mom, saying that she would make her proud.

Rosé developed her passion for singing at a young age after joining a church choir. She practiced throughout her childhood but always saw music as a hobby rather than a career.

THE BEGINNINGS

In 2012, Rosé found out that YG Entertainment were holding auditions in Sydney and flew to the city to take part. It was her father who suggested that she audition, even though Rosé initially thought he was joking.

The audition went well – Rosé ranked first and became a YG Entertainment trainee with immediate effect. It meant that she had to leave college in Australia and move to Seoul, South Korea. It took Rosé four years of training to become a K-pop star, and she has described it as one of the most challenging yet life-changing periods of her life.

Along with the other trainees, Rosé had to constantly prove her worth to Yang Hyun-suk, the label's boss. She took part in tests at the end of every month, where she and the other trainees had to prepare both solo and group song and dance performances. But Rosé's hard work paid off when she was announced as the main vocalist and lead dancer of BLACKPINK. Although she was the last member of the band to be revealed, she was definitely worth the wait.

LEADER OF THE PACK

When Rosé lived in Australia, she was a cheerleader at her school. It's therefore no surprise that she's the group's lead dancer. Her moves stand out from the other girls on stage, and she is able to both dance and hit the high notes required as the main vocalist.

HOMETOWN GIRL

Rosé is Korean but spent so much of her childhood in Melbourne that she views Australia as her home. As she never felt it would be possible to achieve K-pop stardom in the West, she is determined to inspire others.

"I'm just dreaming that one day I'll be able to come back to my home town and perform for everyone."

Rosé's dreams came true during the band's World Tour "In Your Area" when BLACKPINK performed in Australia. In June 2019, Rosé was welcomed home by huge crowds of Aussie fans.

ROSÉ
ROSÉ
ROSÉ
ROSÉ
ROSÉ
ROSÉ
ROSÉ
ROSÉ

DID YOU KNOW?

Ariana Grande sent Rosé a bottle of the "7 Rings" singer's Cloud perfume. Rosé wrote on Instagram, "thank you, Ariana Grande. This is actually the cutest perfume on the planet."

ROSÉ'S DREAMY WORDS

"Enjoy working on your dream, there's nothing better than that."

"I will practice harder and become a great singer."

"It's such a privilege to have a dream."

WHAT DO THE GIRLS SAY ABOUT ROSÉ?

Rosé is mysterious and has a unique sense of humor, which the other girls love. Although she appears shy at first, she likes to laugh at other bandmates' jokes, and Blinks insist that Rosé is an extrovert.

JENNIE

"Rosé is so pretty when she sings and plays guitar at the same time. You will never find this kind of charming voice in Korea."

LISA

"Rosé is the same age as me, and she is my best friend! When I'm with her, I can discuss my problems with her, and there is a big part of me that relies on her as well."

Rosé loves to cook and once said that "tears come to my eyes when I eat really good food."

In 2014, Rosé shared her bucket list with fans. It included wanting to dance with her dad at her wedding.

Rosé believes in the healing power of music: "I search for music I like or interviews by artists I like on YouTube. Watching those videos has a healing effect."

Rosé has a special talent – she can talk even if her mouth is closed.

Rosé hates jokbal – a Korean dish containing pig's feet.

TEN FACTS ABOUT ROSÉ

Rosé has a wide range of hobbies, including drawing, playing the guitar, and riding her bicycle.

Rosé's favorite pizza is topped with pineapple.

Rosé likes watching movies, but only ones with happy endings.

Rosé owns a freshwater parrot fish called Joo-hwang, which means "orange" in Korean.

Rosé is a Christian and regularly attends church.

BEHIND THE SCENES

BLACKPINK DIARIES

The BLACKPINK Diaries are ten-minute videos. They give behind-the-scenes access, including their preparations before and after a concert. The videos are personal, with the girls talking informally, and are mostly filmed on hand-held cameras to make them feel more accessible. All of the episodes have subtitles, descriptions and a running commentary for any new Blinks.

The videos take fans on tour, showing the girls rehearsing, playing instruments, performing on stage, and interacting with fans around the world. They also feature dance practices for the band's "power dance," which is the special dance that the girls do at concerts before their set.

The girls film as a group and individually, allowing fans to get to know their personalities and friendships. Throughout the episodes, fans can also see how the girls grow in confidence both in performing and talking to the camera.

Where to find this?
The "BLACKPINKDIARIES" playlist is on the BLACKPINK YouTube channel.

BLACKPINK HOUSE

These 12-15-minute episodes take fans inside the BLACKPINK house where the girls lived together. The videos show an assortment of different activities – from watching the girls do their laundry and cleaning to seeing them travel the world.

Over the 12 episodes, we see how the house gives the girls more freedom and a safe space to hang out together. Watching the girls cooking together and then sitting around the table and discussing how they are feeling, shows fans how close the girls are – they are friends first, bandmates second.

Where to find this?
The show aired on the South Korean television station, JTBC. The show is also aired online via YouTube and VLIVE.

STAR ROAD

Star Road is a program that allows Korean celebrities to show a different side of their personalities to the ones on stage. It is mostly made up of casual interviews, but it can also contain live footage. Blinks were excited when it was announced that BLACKPINK would star in 24 guest episodes. Each episode is around five minutes long and has a different theme – from singing breakup songs and playing games to answering questions from fans. The girls open up, have fun and also get to know each other more. This honest, authentic content is exactly what Blinks cherish and allows them to feel connected to the girls.

Where to find this?
All videos can be found on VLIVE.TV and the VLIVE app.

LISA

"Enjoy living life to the fullest."

Name:
Lalisa Manoban /
Pranpriya Manoban

Also known as:
Lisa, Lalice, Laliz, Pokpak

Date of birth:
March 27th, 1997

Star sign:
Aries

Birthplace:
Bangkok, Thailand

Height:
5 feet, 5 inches

Education:
Praphamontree II School,
Thailand

Languages:
Korean, Japanese, English,
Thai, basic Chinese

Early career:
Became a YG Entertainment
trainee in 2010 after an
audition in Thailand

Joined BLACKPINK:
Second member to be revealed
on June 8th, 2016

> **"Lisa has been learning various kinds of dances. She participated in a dance competition in Thailand, *To Be Number One*, and went on to participate on *LG Entertainer* as one of We Zaa Cool Team."**
>
> – *Hallyu K Star* interview, 2016

LISA
LISA
LISA
LISA
LISA
LISA
LISA
LISA

> **"Lisa is so cheerful, friendly, funny, and she always respects older people. She has long arms and legs, so whatever she wears, she looks good."**
>
> – *Hallyu K Star* interview, 2016

EARLY DAYS

Lisa, whose birth name is Pranpriya Manoban, was born in Bangkok, Thailand. She later legally changed her first name to Lalisa, which means "the one who was praised." Lisa discovered this when she visited a fortune teller who told her that her new name would bring her luck.

Lisa's stepfather is Marco Bruschweiler, a very famous Swiss chef who is currently based in Thailand. He runs a renowned Thai cooking school, which explains why Lisa is such a big foodie. As a child, Lisa attended Praphamontree II School and loved dancing and rapping. She has an older sister who, during an interview with a K-pop news outlet *Hallyu K Star*, described how Lisa entered dance competitions from a young age.

THE BEGINNINGS

Lisa was only just a teenager when she auditioned to become a trainee with YG Entertainment. In 2011, YG Entertainment held a competition in Thailand for the first time, and Lisa submitted a dance video. The audition was demanding, and Lisa's sister has said how much energy — both physical and mental — Lisa put in to it.

Lisa was delighted when she ranked first place and was offered a trainee position by Yang Hyun-suk. It was made even more special when she found out that she was the only person from Thailand to be accepted in 2011. Later that year, she moved to South Korea to begin her formal training.

Lisa trained for five years before making her debut and, despite being the "maknae" (the youngest member of a K-pop group), her commitment to her career was clear. In 2016, she joined BLACKPINK as the group's main dancer and lead rapper. Lisa was the second member of the group to be revealed and became the first non-Korean YG Entertainment artist.

"BLACKPINK isn't possible if we aren't four."

THAI PRINCESS

In Thailand, Lisa is referred to as a "Thai princess" by Blinks, and she is the band's unofficial ambassador for Thai culture. Jennie frequently mentions how Lisa knows the best places to get the most authentic Thai food.

PURR-FECT COMPANION

Lisa loves the company of cats, especially her own super-cute one called Leo, who she adores. She celebrated his birthday in February 2019 by posting a card for him on Instagram.

"After I finish work for the day, I go back to the dorm and see my cat waiting for me and feel happy."

LISA
LISA
LISA
LISA
LISA
LISA
LISA
LISA

DID YOU KNOW?

During a VLIVE broadcast in 2017, it was announced that Lisa's nickname is LaLi Con Artist due to her frequent cheating at board games.

FUTUREWEAR

LISA'S WORDS OF WISDOM

"Be yourself and have confidence, show them all your charms."

"Have fun and live life."

"When I'm feeling nervous, I encourage myself by saying, 'I'll be fine, I can do it.'"

WHAT DO THE GIRLS SAY ABOUT LISA?

Lisa is often described as the band's "happy pill" and is a fun, playful member of the group. She makes the best "cutesy" facial expressions.

JISOO

"She usually wakes up and eats chocolates and potato chips beside her bed, then goes back to sleep."

ROSÉ

"Lisa is so pretty, sometimes I worry that I might be compared to her if I stand beside her. Her character is so nice – sometimes naughty and so bright."

Lisa is fluent in four languages – she can speak Korean, English, and Japanese, as well as her native Thai.

Lisa strongly dislikes rude people and always tries to be nice to everyone.

Lisa's favorite flowers are pink roses.

If Lisa could be any Disney princess, she would be Rapunzel.

Lisa eats snacks in her room constantly. Lisa admits she's too lazy to get up and go to the kitchen for food, so she has mini fridge in her room!

TEN FACTS ABOUT LISA

In 2019, Lisa was announced as the muse for Hedi Slimane, the current artistic director of luxury French fashion label Céline.

Lisa has dreams of one day opening a Thai restaurant in Korea as she is "disappointed at the fact that people have no idea how delicious Thai rice noodles are!"

Lisa loves the number 27 because it's the date of her birthday.

If Lisa won a million dollars she would travel all around the world.

Lisa became the first K-pop female idol to achieve 2 million likes on a social media post in just 48 hours.

TIMELINE

Take a look at some of BLACKPINK's greatest moments over the years.

2010-2012

♥ **August 2010:** Jennie signs as a trainee with YG Entertainment.

♥ **April 2011:** Lisa signs as a trainee with YG Entertainment after sailing through the auditions. She becomes the first non-Korean artist to sign with YG.

♥ **July 2011:** Jisoo signs as a trainee after being scouted by a casting agent at a YG Entertainment concert.

♥ **May 2012:** Rosé signs as a trainee with YG Entertainment.

2016

♥ **June 29th:** YG Entertainment reveals the final line-up and the name of the group – BLACKPINK.

♥ **August 8th:** BLACKPINK's debut single album *Square One* is released. Its two lead singles chart at number one and two on *Billboard's* World Digital Songs Chart. BLACKPINK is the fastest act to achieve this and the third Korean artist or group to hold the top two positions.

♥ **August 14th:** BLACKPINK's first music show performance is aired on SBS's *Inkigayo*. They break the record for the shortest time for a girl group to win a music program, taking first place just 13 days after their debut.

♥ **November 1st:** BLACKPINK releases their second single album *Square Two* with the lead singles "Playing with Fire" and "Stay." "Playing with Fire" becomes their second single to hit number one on *Billboard's* World Digital Songs Chart.

2017

♥ **January 17th:** BLACKPINK names their fan club "Blink," a blend of "black" and "pink."

♥ **May 5th:** BLACKPINK becomes ambassadors for Incheon Main Customs in South Korea.

♥ **June 22nd:** BLACKPINK releases a digital single titled "As If It's Your Last." It debuts at number one on *Billboard's* World Digital Song Chart after only one day, making it their third number-one hit on the chart. The music video for the song later went on to break the record for the most-liked music video by a female K-pop group on YouTube.

♥ **November 20th:** BLACKPINK holds a showcase at Nippon Budokan in Tokyo. More than 14,000 people attend and, reportedly, around 200,000 people try to get tickets.

2018

♥ **June 15ᵗʰ**: BLACKPINK releases their first EP, *Square Up*. The single "Ddu-Du Ddu-Du" debuts at number 17 on the Official Trending Chart in the UK, making them the first female K-pop group to enter the chart since its launch in 2016.

♥ **June 21ˢᵗ**: "Ddu-Du Ddu-Du" continues to rise. The single debuts as the highest-charting Hot 100 hit ever by an all-female K-pop act, opening at number 55 with 12.4 million US streams and 7,000 downloads.

♥ **July 28ᵗʰ**: BLACKPINK ranks first for brand reputation based on analysis by the Korea Institute of Corporate Reputation.

♥ **October 19ᵗʰ**: BLACKPINK collaborates with English singer Dua Lipa on "Kiss and Make Up." It peaks at number 36 in the UK Singles Chart, marking BLACKPINK's first Top 40 entry. This makes them the first female K-pop group and third Korean act overall to reach the chart's Top 40.

2019

♥ **January 21ˢᵗ**: The music video for "Ddu-Du Ddu-Du" becomes the most-viewed music video by a K-pop group on YouTube, with 620.9 million views.

♥ **February 9ᵗʰ**: BLACKPINK makes their debut US performance at Universal Music Group's Grammy Artist Showcase.

♥ **February 28ᵗʰ**: BLACKPINK becomes the first female K-pop group to grace the cover of *Billboard* magazine.

♥ **April 5ᵗʰ**: BLACKPINK's second EP, *Kill This Love*, is released. The single "Kill This Love" peaks at number two in South Korea and becomes the best-charting song of a South Korean girl group in the United States. It was the fastest music video by a K-pop group to reach 400 million views and currently has over 500 million views on YouTube. This song also appears in a 2020 dance video game, *Just Dance*.

♥ **April 12ᵗʰ**: BLACKPINK becomes the first female K-pop group to perform at Coachella Festival.

2020

♥ **February 22ⁿᵈ**: BLACKPINK finishes their 2019/20 World Tour "In Your Area" with an epic performance in Fukuoka, Japan.

DID YOU KNOW?

BLACKPINK had a prime spot at Coachella and were placed on the second line of the poster.

K-BEAUTY

Jisoo, Jennie, Rosé, and Lisa use an eight-step skincare routine in the morning and a ten-step skincare routine in the evening to keep their skin looking healthy and beautiful.

It's an extensive routine, but Korean skincare is all about layering to nourish the skin. Each step has its own significant role to keep skin looking glowing and dewy.

BLACKPINK's morning routine

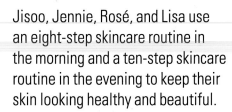

Step 1: Wash face with water

First thing in the morning, skin is cleansed with water. Water removes the impurities that settle on the face overnight.

Step 2: Toner

Hydration is the key to flawless, radiant skin; without a toner, skin can become dry and dehydrated. Toner is also used to balance the skin's pH levels.

Step 3: Essence

Essence is a cross between a toner and a serum. It's great for hydrating the complexion and giving a youthful appearance.

Step 4: Ampoule

An ampoule is a super-charged serum with a higher concentration of active ingredients. It's perfect for when the skin is having a crisis – an ampoule gives it the boost it needs.

Step 5: Serum

Serum targets specific skin concerns such as dehydration or tired, dull-looking skin.

Step 6: Eye cream

An eye cream is applied to protect and hydrate the delicate eye area. It also reduces any puffiness around the eyes that can be caused by lack of sleep.

Step 7: Moisturizer

A soothing moisturizer is used in a light layer across the skin for long-lasting, all-day hydration.

Step 8: Sunscreen

Sunscreen protects the face from UV rays, which can cause dark spots and wrinkles to develop.

BLACKPINK's evening routine

Jisoo, Jennie, Rosé, and Lisa let each product absorb properly between the steps and are very gentle with their skin. The girls understand that it is important to choose products with ingredients that work well with their skin and, as they all have different skin types, they use a wide range of products.

Step 1: Oil-based cleanser

An oil-based cleanser is used to remove the buildup of dirt and any makeup that may be on the face.

Step 2: Double-cleansing

A water-based cleanser gently removes the oil residue and water-based impurities from the day.

Step 3: Exfoliate

Using a gentle enzyme exfoliator removes the dead skin cells. The girls only do this step twice a week as over-exfoliation can be harsh on the skin.

Step 4: Toning

Toning happens in the evening as well as the morning as it provides a base layer of hydration, making the skin more amenable to what's about to go on top.

Step 5: Essence

Essence is used after a toner to add another layer of hydration before the serum is applied.

Step 6: Ampoule

Ampoules are used again before bed to help firm and hydrate tired-looking skin and to add hydration and radiance.

Step 7: Serum

A healing facial night serum means bright and glowing skin in the morning.

Step 8: Sheet mask

The girls routinely use sheet masks before going to bed to keep their skin moist and supple.

Step 9: Eye cream

An eye cream is applied again to continue the protection and hydration of the delicate eye area. Eye creams can also help eliminate dark circles.

Step 10: Moisturizer

Night is an essential time to renew the skin, and using a moisturizer before bed creates softer, more hydrated skin the next day.

BLACKPINK's hairstyles

BLACKPINK has made waves by sporting creative and iconic hairstyles since their debut. Here are some of their best hairstyles over the years.

JENNIE'S BLONDE HAIR

Jennie swapped her signature brunette locks in 2019 for a new color — Barbie blonde. She showed off her new look in the "Kill This Love" teaser where she stares into the camera with long, bright-blonde waves.

This was a dramatic makeover as Jennie had kept her hair more or less dark up until then. She'd experimented with purple extensions, and occasionally blonde highlights, but this was the first time she went for all-over platinum blonde.

LISA'S EVER-CHANGING HAIR COLOR

While Lisa's hairstyle hasn't changed a huge amount since her debut, she keeps it fresh and fun by changing the color.

Lisa has gone from brunette to pink to neon yellow, but one of her most out-there looks was the combination of pastel blue and silver on her fringe. This icy balayage was the perfect inspiration for the wintry months.

Whatever the color of Lisa's hair, it always matches her outfits perfectly.

ROSÉ'S BEAUTIFUL BRAIDS

Rosé is different from the other girls. While they continuously change their hairstyles – from bangs to braids and bob cuts to bunches – Rosé has stayed loyal to her signature hair-down look. This is a beautiful, elegant style and one that suits the main vocalist of the band. However, in 2018, Rosé shocked Blinks with a bold new design.

When the band performed "Forever Young" on *Show! Music Core*, Rosé came on stage with her hair in French braids. Blinks expressed their excitement at her fresh, stylish look and cannot wait to see if Rosé experiments with other hairstyles in the future.

JISOO'S FAIRY TALE LOOK

Jisoo has rocked soft, dark colors over the years – mainly browns, blacks, and reds. These rich, ombre tones became her signature look. But Jisoo went for a brighter color in 2017 and surprised Blinks by dying her hair purple. This new style was to promote "As If It's Your Last," and it was the first time that Jisoo had sported purple hair since the band's debut. Many Blinks loved the new, enchanting style and said that it looked like she belonged in a fairy tale. This feeling intensified after Jisoo was seen wearing a tiara and a flower crown.

Stylist sensations

BLACKPINK has had the same stylist, Choi Kyung-won, since their debut in 2016. In an interview with *WWD* in 2018, Choi spoke about the group's style. She had a bold vision for the band – she wanted to create a new style milestone and for their look to be at the height of women's fashion in South Korea.

YG Entertainment were also keen for the girls to be different from other groups and to have a distinctive look. For Choi, the secret was to compose a style that reflected each girl's personality but also ensured they looked like one harmonious group.

Dress like BLACKPINK

If you want to dress in the style of BLACKPINK then think luxury fashion – but with an edge. Lavish creations from Alexander McQueen, Balenciaga, and Charles Jeffrey Loverboy had never been worn by a female K-pop group before. These girls dress in them as naturally as if they are everyday brands.

The girls became the first female K-pop group to combine luxury fashion brands with underground Japanese street labels. They have created fashion trends in South Korea – from school skirts to diamanté belts – so it's no surprise that BLACKPINK have been described as the embodiment of women's fashion.

QUICK QUESTION
Which member of BLACKPINK had 22 costume changes in a three-minute music video?

Answer: Jennie in her solo song, 'Solo'. What a fashion queen!

JISOO

Jisoo loves bright colors and pulled off a combination of pastel green and neon pink in an Adidas sponsorship post in 2018. She experiments with accessories and is always adorned with sparkly earrings, geometric bangles, and floral-embellished nails. Jisoo has a soft, feminine style and is known as "Miss Korea" by Blinks.

According to *Vogue Korea*, Jennie is the group's "Human Chanel" due to her love of luxury brands. Nothing screams Chanel more than its iconic tweed, which is what Jennie wore to the Chanel Spring/Summer 2019 show. She's often seen with her Chanel 2.55 bag, along with other classic high-end handbags.

JENNIE

ROSÉ

Rosé's look is simple, which makes her the most relatable style icon of the group. She is a minimalist and keeps it classy with monochrome, basic colors and minimal accessories. However she is not afraid to wear prints and florals – these are often reserved for music videos or when she is on stage – and when she does, she keeps it classic.

Lisa's style is quirky but always on trend. She is often found walking the red carpet, and it is here that she mixes up her style with a striking statement accessory. Lisa loves oversized everything – from jeans and jumpers to coats and chunky sneakers.

LISA

ULTIMATE QUIZ

It's time to test your knowledge in this ultimate quiz. Do you know BLACKPINK well enough to answer the 20 questions below? Find out your true fan status by checking your answers on **page 60**.

1. When the girls sat down with Apple Music's Brooke Reese in 2019, which three artists did they reveal to be their most desired collaborators?

....

2. Jennie claimed she had a special talent before it was debunked. What was this talent?

....

3. When was BLACKPINK's second single album, *Square Two,* released?

....

4. Which girl became the first K-pop female artist to get 20 million followers on Instagram?

....

5. Which is Jisoo's favorite Pokémon?

....

6. What country was the group's first showcase held in?

....

7. What is Jennie's star sign?

....

8. What was the first song BLACKPINK performed at Coachella in 2019?

....

9. Which song are the following lyrics from: "Like the flames that burn without a sound, I hope you kiss me like it's our last"? And who sings that verse?

....

10. Which duo posted a photo with three of the girls with the caption "Fell in love 3 times last night?"

....

11. Which girl was caught playing with a water bottle on
her shoulder during the Seoul Music Awards?

....

12. In the "Boombayah" music video, which girl blows a bubble with chewing gum?

....

13. In an interview with *Zipper*, what word did Rosé use to describe her personality?

....

14. What does Lisa do on her days off?

....

15. What is Lisa's favorite track to sing at karaoke?

....

16. On the variety program *Weekly Idol*, Rosé said that
MC Jeong Hyeong-don reminded her of who?

....

17. Which girl can speak the most languages?

....

18. In a *Billboard* interview, the girls played "How Well Do You Know Your
Bandmates?" Which girl was voted the most likely to take a selfie?

....

19. Which girl received an onstage marriage proposal?

....

20. Which song are the following lyrics from: "I'm so bad at this,
won't you set me free?" And who sings that verse?

....

THE FUTURE

"BLACKPINK are global superstars in the making," said John Janick, the Chairman and CEO of Universal Music Group, when YG Entertainment and Interscope Records announced a global partnership in 2018.

"**The music and visuals are immediately striking and so different from anything else happening in pop music. We are beyond excited to partner with YG in pursuit of their vision for BLACKPINK world domination.**"

— John Janick, 2018

2019 looked like BLACKPINK's wildest, most successful year yet. The girls sold out arenas in London, Paris, and Berlin, took to the stage at Coachella, launched solo projects, and broke music records worldwide. But it seems the best is yet to come in 2020 and beyond. The band's producer, Teddy Park, has suggested that they have many forthcoming, top-secret adventures lined up overseas.

"**Entertainment today is more global than ever. Music and real talent transcends culture, language, and really has no boundaries.**"

— Teddy Park, 2018

ULTIMATE QUIZ: THE ANSWERS

1. Billie Eilish, Tyga, Halsey
   ♥
2. Eating potato chips silently
   ♥
3. November 1st, 2016
   ♥
4. Lisa
   ♥
5. Pikachu
   ♥
6. Japan
   ♥
7. Capricorn
   ♥

8. "Ddu-Du Ddu-Du"
   ♥
9. "Forever Young," Jisoo
   ♥
10. The Chainsmokers
    ♥
11. Jisoo
    ♥
12. Jennie
    ♥
13. Sensitive
    ♥
14. Sleep
    ♥

15. "You Belong With Me" by Taylor Swift
    ♥
16. Her father
    ♥
17. Lisa — she can speak five languages
    ♥
18. Jisoo
    ♥
19. Jennie
    ♥
20. "As If It's Your Last," Rosé
    ♥

YG Entertainment also revealed through Instagram that solo projects will be a big part of the group's work over the coming years.

"**We are simultaneously working on new BLACK-PINK songs as well as solo projects for all four members at the moment. The biggest strength of BLACKPINK is that each member's ability as a solo artist is as strong as their teamwork/cohesiveness.**"
– YG Entertainment, 2018

Whatever the future holds, the girls have their own messages to spread. Whether they're symbolizing female empowerment or encouraging fans to be unapologetically themselves, BLACKPINK strike a chord with Blinks around the world. This is sure to make them relatable and adored for a long time to come.

DID YOU KNOW?

BLACKPINK was nominated for MTV's Hottest Summer Superstar 2019. Other nominees included BTS, Ariana Grande, and Taylor Swift.